Worship Band Edition

PLAYBACK+
Speed • Pitch • Balance • Loop

Contemporary Worship Classics

To access audio visit:
www.halleonard.com/mylibrary

Enter Code
5586-0625-9014-7245

ISBN 978-1-4950-3464-0

7777 W. BLUEMOUND RD. P.O. BOX 13819 MILWAUKEE, WI 53213

Visit Hal Leonard Online at
www.halleonard.com

www.praisecharts.com

PREFACE

PraiseCharts was started in 1998 by Ryan Dahl, a worship pastor who was striving to develop a team of young musicians, but struggling to find sheet music that kept pace with current trends in music and technology. Today, PraiseCharts has become an invaluable resource for worship leaders around the world, as they tap into a growing online catalog of more than 15,000 worship songs. PraiseCharts is entirely virtual as a company, and yet very personal, practical, tangible and connected. Ryan leads a global team of talented arrangers, transcribers, producers and administrators who desire to make contemporary worship music available to churches worldwide. He lives and works from his home in Langley, British Columbia (Canada), alongside his wife and four children.

LEAD SHEETS

CHORD CHARTS

RHYTHM CHARTS

Amazing Grace
(My Chains Are Gone)

Lead Sheet
(SAT)

Words by John Newton
Traditional American Melody
Additional Words and Music by Chris Tomlin and Louie Giglio
Arranged by Dan Galbraith

Forever

Lead Sheet
(SAT)

Words and Music by Chris Tomlin
Arranged by Dan Galbraith

Modern rock ♩ = 84

A²   F♯m7(4)

E   D²   1   2

1. Give

1 Verse   *mf* A²

thanks to the Lord,____ our God and____ King.____ His

love en-dures____ for-ev -____ er.____ For He is good,____ He is a- D²

bove all____ things.____ His love en-dures____ for-ev -____ er.____ Sing A

praise,_____ E   sing____ praise!____ D²/F♯

2 Verse   A²   *mf*

2. With a might-y hand____ and out-stretched____ arm,____ His
3. From the ris - ing to the set - ting____ sun,____ His

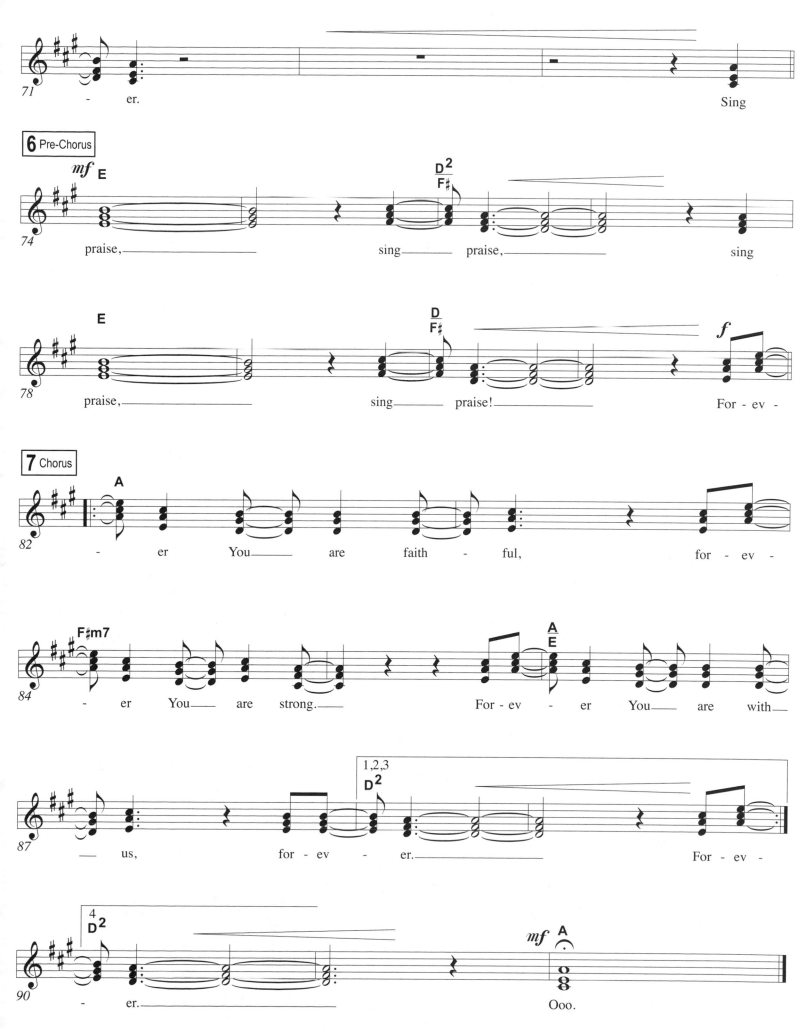

Lead Sheet
(SAT)

God of Wonders

Words and Music by Marc Byrd and Steve Hindalong
Arranged by Dan Galbraith and Dave Iula

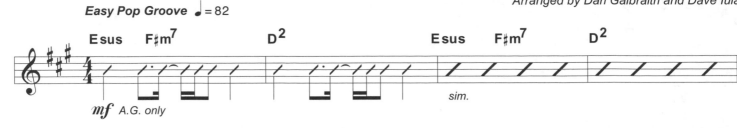

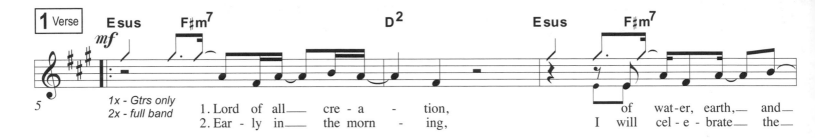

1. Lord of all cre-a-tion, of wat-er, earth, and
2. Ear-ly in the morn-ing, I will cel-e-brate the

— sky, the heav-ens are Your tab-er-na-cle;
— light, and when I stum-ble in the dark-ness,

glo-ry to the Lord on high. God of won-ders be-yond our gal-ax-
I will call Your name by night.

y, You are ho-ly, ho-ly! The

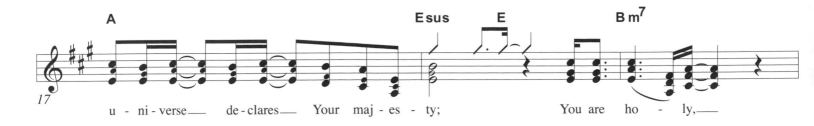

u-ni-verse de-clares Your maj-es-ty; You are ho-ly,

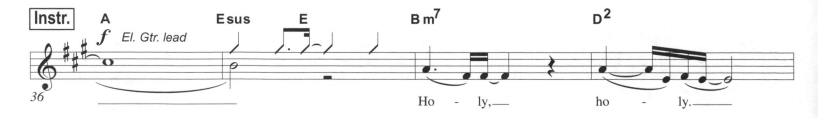

Instr.

f El. Gtr. lead

36

Ho - ly,—— ho - ly.——

40

Ho - ly,—— Lord.——

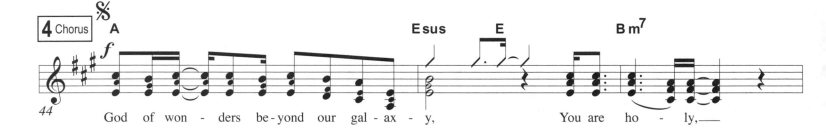

4 Chorus

f

44

God of won - ders be - yond our gal - ax - y, You are ho - ly,——

47

ho - ly!—— The u - ni - verse—— de - clares—— Your maj - es -

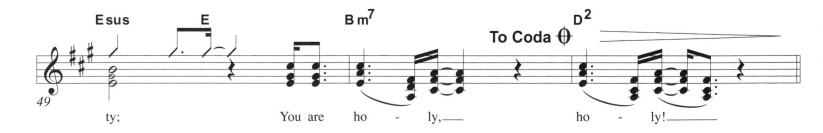

To Coda

49

ty; You are ho - ly,—— ho - ly!

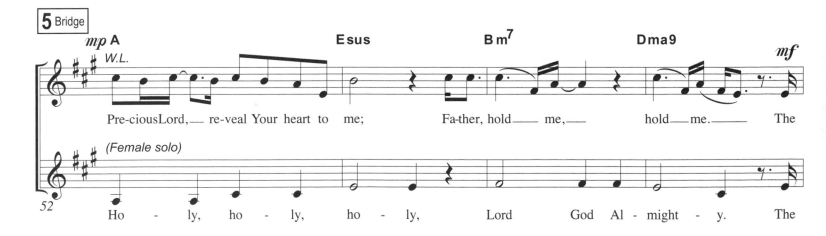

5 Bridge

mp W.L. *mf*

52

Pre-cious Lord,— re-veal Your heart to me; Fa-ther, hold—— me,—— hold—— me. The

(Female solo)

Ho - ly, ho - ly, ho - ly, Lord God Al - might - y. The

W.L. **A** **E sus**

u - ni - verse___ de - clares___ Your ma - jes - ty; You are

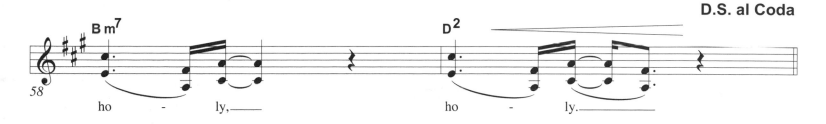

D.S. al Coda

B m7 **D2**

ho - ly,___ ho - ly.___

CODA **D2** **B m7** **Dma9**

ho - ly,___ You are ho - ly,___ ho - ly.

Tag *f* **B m7** *W.L.* **D add2**

...to the Lord of heav - en and___ earth,___

P.T.

Hal - le - lu - jah,___

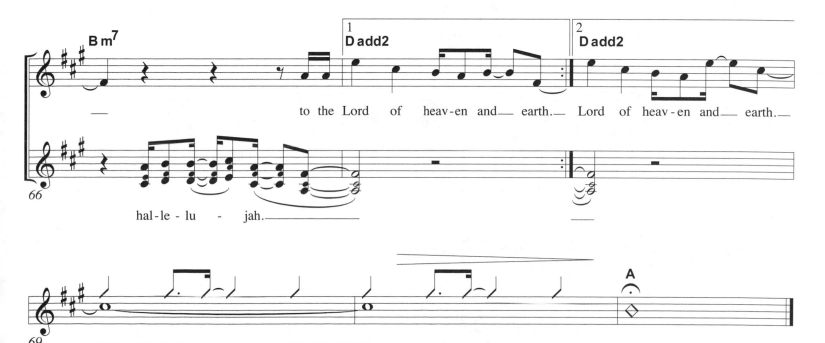

B m7 1. **D add2** 2. **D add2**

to the Lord of heav - en and___ earth.___ Lord of heav - en and___ earth.___

hal - le - lu - jah.___

A

Lead Sheet
(SAT)

Here I Am to Worship
(Light of the World)

Words and Music by Tim Hughes
Arranged by Dan Galbraith

Medium ballad ♩ = 76

1. Light of the world, You stepped down into darkness, opened my eyes, let me see.
2. King of all days, oh, so highly exalted, glorious in heaven above.

Beauty that made this heart adore You,
Humbly you came to the earth You created.

hope of a life spent with You.
All for love's sake became poor.

Here I am to worship, here I am to bow down, here I am to say that You're my God.

You're altogether lovely, altogether worthy, altogether

1 - Repeat to Verse

wonderful to me.

I'll nev-

Holy Is the Lord

Lead Sheet
(SAT)

Words and Music by Chris Tomlin
and Louie Giglio
Arranged by Dan Galbraith

Blessed Be Your Name

Lead Sheet
(SAT)

Words and Music by Matt Redman and Beth Redman
Arranged by Dan Galbraith and Shane Ohlson

Mighty to Save

Lead Sheet
(SAT)

**Words and Music by Ben Fielding
and Reuben Morgan**
Arranged by Dan Galbraith

In Christ Alone

Lead Sheet
(SAT)

**Words and Music by Keith Getty
and Stuart Townend**
Arranged by Dan Galbraith

4. No guilt in

life, no fear in death, this is the pow'r of Christ in

me; From life's first cry to fi - nal breath, Je - sus com-

mands my des - ti - ny; No pow'r of hell, no scheme of

man can ev - er pluck me from His hand; 'Til He re-

turns or calls me home, here in the pow'r of Christ I'll stand.

Sing to the King

Lead Sheet
(SAT)

Words and Music by Billy James Foote
Arranged by Dan Galbraith

Your Name

Lead Sheet
(SAT)

Words and Music by Paul Baloche
and Glenn Packiam
Arranged by Dan Galbraith

Amazing Grace (My Chains Are Gone)

Words by John Newton
Traditional American Melody
Additional Words and Music by Chris Tomlin and Louie Giglio

Key: Eb · Tempo: 62
CCLI Song No. 4768151

Intro (2x)

Eb5 / / / | **Eb2** / / /

Verse 1

   Eb2   **Ebsus** **Eb2**   **Bb/Eb**
A - mazing grace how sweet the sound that saved a wretch like me
  Eb2   **Eb2/G** **Ab2**   **Eb2**   **Bb/Eb Eb2**
I once was   lost   but now I'm found, was blind but now I see

Verse 2

    Eb2   **Ebsus** **Eb2**   **Bb/Eb**
'Twas grace that taught my heart to fear and grace my fears re - lieved
  Eb2   **Eb2/G** **Ab2**   **Eb2**   **Bb/Eb**   **Eb2 Ab/Eb Eb**
How precious   did   that grace ap - pear the hour I   first   be - lieved

Chorus

        Ab2   **Eb2/G**   **Ab2**   **Eb2/G**
My chains are gone I've been set free, my God my Savior has ransomed   me
    Ab2   **Eb2/G**   **Fm7 Bbsus**   **Eb5**
And like a flood His mercy rains   unending love   amazing grace

Intro (2x)

Verse 3

   Eb2   **Ebsus** **Eb2**   **Bb/Eb**
The Lord has promised good to me, His word my hope se - cures
  Eb2   **Eb2/G** **Ab2**   **Eb2**   **Bb/Eb**   **Eb2 Ab/Eb Eb**
He will my shield and portion be as long as   life   en - dures

Chorus (2x)

Verse 4

  Eb2   **Ebsus** **Eb2**   **Bb/Eb**
The earth shall soon dis - solve like snow, the sun forbear to shine
  Eb2   **Eb2/G** **Ab2**   **Eb2**   **Bb/Eb Eb** **Ebsus**
But God who called me here be - low will be for - ever   mine
  Eb2   **Bb/Eb Eb** **Ebsus Eb2**   **Bb/Eb Eb2**
Will be for - ever   mine You   are for - ever   mine

Amazing Grace (My Chains Are Gone) (CAPO 1)

Words by John Newton
Traditional American Melody
Additional Words and Music by Chris Tomlin and Louie Giglio

Key: D · Capo: 1 (Eb) · Tempo: 62
CCLI Song No. 4768151

Intro (2x)
D5 / / / | D2 / / /

Verse 1

D2   Dsus D2   A/D
A - mazing grace how sweet the sound that saved a wretch like me
 D2 D2/F# G2   D2   A/D D2
I once was lost but now I'm found, was blind but now I see

Verse 2

D2   Dsus D2   A/D
'Twas grace that taught my heart to fear and grace my fears re - lieved
 D2 D2/F# G2   D2   A/D D2 G/D D
How precious did that grace ap - pear the hour I first be - lieved

Chorus

      G2   D2/F#   G2   D2/F#
My chains are gone I've been set free, my God my Savior has ransomed me
     G2   D2/F#   Em7 Asus   D5
And like a flood His mercy rains unending love   amazing grace

Intro (2x)

Verse 3

D2   Dsus D2   A/D
The Lord has promised good to me, His word my hope se - cures
 D2 D2/F# G2   D2   A/D D2 G/D D
He will my shield and portion be as long as life en - dures

Chorus (2x)

Verse 4

D2   Dsus D2   A/D
The earth shall soon dis - solve like snow, the sun forbear to shine
 D2 D2/F# G2   D2   A/D D Dsus
But God who called me here be - low will be for - ever mine
 D2 A/D D Dsus D2 A/D D2
Will be for - ever mine You are for - ever mine

D5 D2 Dsus A/D D2/F# G2 G/D D Em7 Asus

Amazing Grace (My Chains Are Gone) (CAPO 3)

Words by John Newton
Traditional American Melody
Additional Words and Music by Chris Tomlin and Louie Giglio

Key: C · Capo: 3 (Eb) · Tempo: 62
CCLI Song No. 4768151

Intro (2x)
C5 / / / | C2 / / /

Verse 1
  C2   Csus   C2   G/C
A - mazing grace how sweet the sound that saved a wretch like me
 C2   C2/E   F2   C2   G/C C2
I once was lost but now I'm found, was blind but now I see

Verse 2
   C2   Csus   C2   G/C
'Twas grace that taught my heart to fear and grace my fears re - lieved
  C2   C2/E   F2   C2   G/C   C2   F/C C
How precious did that grace ap - pear the hour I first be - lieved

Chorus
             F2   C2/E   F2   C2/E
My chains are gone I've been set free, my God my Savior has ransomed me
     F2   C2/E   Dm7 Gsus   C5
And like a flood His mercy rains unending love amazing grace

Intro (2x)

Verse 3
  C2   Csus   C2   G/C
The Lord has promised good to me, His word my hope se - cures
 C2   C2/E   F2   C2   G/C   C2   F/C C
He will my shield and portion be as long as life en - dures

Chorus (2x)

Verse 4
  C2   Csus   C2   G/C
The earth shall soon dis - solve like snow, the sun forbear to shine
 C2   C2/E   F2   C2   G/C C   Csus
But God who called me here be - low will be for - ever mine
 C2   G/C C   Csus C2   G/C C2
Will be for - ever mine You are for - ever mine

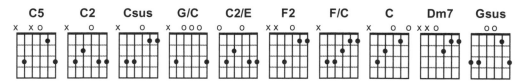

Chord diagrams: C5, C2, Csus, G/C, C2/E, F2, F/C, C, Dm7, Gsus

This page is intentionally left blank
to avoid unnecessary page turns.

Blessed Be Your Name

Words and Music by Matt Redman and Beth Redman

Key: A · Tempo: 123
CCLI Song No. 3798438

Intro
A5 / / / | / / / / | / / / / | / / / /

Verse 1
```
A          E              F#m7      D2
  Blessed be Your name in the  land  that is plentiful
              A          E         D2
Where Your streams of a - bundance flow, blessed be Your name
A          E              F#m7      D2
  Blessed be Your name when I'm found in the desert place
              A          E         D2
Though I walk through the wilderness, blessed be Your name
```

Pre-Chorus
```
A          E              F#m7          D2
  Every blessing You pour out I'll      turn back to praise
A          E              F#m7          D2
  When the darkness closes in Lord,       still I will say
```

Chorus
```
            A          E                F#m7 D
Blessed be the name of the Lord, Blessed be Your  name
            A          E                F#m7 E    D
Blessed be the name of the Lord, Blessed be Your  glo - rious name
```

Verse 2
```
A          E              F#m7      D2
  Blessed be Your name when the sun's shining down on me
              A      E         D2
When the world's all as it should be, blessed be Your name
A          E              F#m7          D
  Blessed be Your name on the road  marked with suffering
              A      E         D2
Though there's pain in the offering, blessed be Your name
```

Pre-Chorus > Chorus (2x)

Bridge (2x)
```
  A          E      F#m7          D
You give and take a - way, You  give  and take a -way
  A          E      F#m7          D2
My heart will choose to say Lord blessed be Your name
```

Chorus (2x) > Intro (2x)

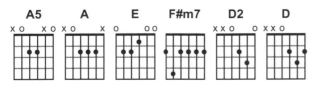

Blessed Be Your Name (CAPO 2)

Words and Music by Matt Redman and Beth Redman

Key: G · Capo: 2 (A) · Tempo: 123
CCLI Song No. 3798438

Intro
G5 / / / / | / / / / | / / / / | / / / /

Verse 1
G   D   Em7   C2
  Blessed be Your name in the land that is plentiful
                    G   D   C2
Where Your streams of a - bundance flow, blessed be Your name
G   D   Em7   C2
  Blessed be Your name when I'm found in the desert place
                G   D   C2
Though I walk through the wilderness, blessed be Your name

Pre-Chorus
G   D   Em7   C2
  Every blessing You pour out I'll   turn back to praise
G   D   Em7   C2
  When the darkness closes in Lord,   still I will say

Chorus
              G   D   Em7   C
Blessed be the name of the Lord, Blessed be Your name
              G   D   Em7 D   C
Blessed be the name of the Lord, Blessed be Your glo - rious name

Verse 2
G   D   Em7   C2
  Blessed be Your name when the sun's shining down on me
                G   D   C2
When the world's all as it should be, blessed be Your name
G   D   Em7   C
  Blessed be Your name on the road marked with suffering
                    G   D   C2
Though there's pain in the offering, blessed be Your name

Pre-Chorus > Chorus (2x)

Bridge (2x)
      G   D   Em7   C
You give and take a - way, You give and take a -way
      G   D   Em7   C2
My heart will choose to say Lord blessed be Your name

Chorus (2x) > Intro (2x)

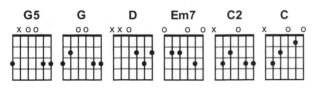

Forever

Words and Music by
Chris Tomlin

Key: A · Tempo: 124
CCLI Song No. 3148428

Intro (2x)
```
A / / / / | / / / / | F#m7 / / / | / / / /
E / / / / | / / / / | D2 / / / | / / / /
```

Verse 1
    A2
Give thanks to the Lord our God and King, His love endures forever
D2   **A**
For He is good He is above all things, His love endures for - ever
      E   **D2/F#**
Sing praise, sing praise

Verse 2
A2
    With a mighty hand and outstretched arm, His love endures forever
D2   **A**
    For the life that's been reborn, His love endures for - ever
      E   **D2/F#**   **E**   **D2/F#**
Sing praise, sing praise, sing praise, sing praise

Chorus 1
    A   **F#m7**
For - ever God is faithful, for - ever God is strong
    E   **D2**   **A2**
For - ever God is with us, for - ever for - ever

Verse 3
A2
    From the rising to the setting sun, His love endures forever
    D2   **A**
By the grace of God we will carry on, His love endures for - ever

Pre-Chorus
| E | D2/F# | E | D2/F# |

Sing praise, sing praise, sing praise, sing praise

Chorus 2

    A   F#m7

For - ever God is faithful, for - ever God is strong

    E   D2

For - ever God is with us, for - ever, and ever and ever

    A   F#m7

For - ever God is faithful, for - ever God is strong

    E   D2   A2

For - ever God is with us, for - ever, forever, for - ever

Tag

A2

Give thanks to the Lord for He is good, give thanks to the Lord for He is good

His love endures forever, His love endures forever, His love endures forever

Pre-Chorus

Chorus 3

    A   F#m7

For - ever You are faithful, for - ever You are strong

    A/E   D2

For - ever You are with us, for - ever

    A   F#m7

For - ever You are faithful, for - ever You are strong

    A/E   D2 A

For - ever You are with us, for - ever Ooo

Forever (CAPO 2)

Words and Music by
Chris Tomlin

Key: G · Capo: 2 (A) · Tempo: 124
CCLI Song No. 3148428

Intro (2x)

G / / / | / / / / | Em7 / / / | / / / /
D / / / | / / / / | C2 / / / | / / / /

Verse 1

G2
Give thanks to the Lord our God and King, His love endures forever
C2   G
For He is good He is above all things, His love endures for - ever
        D   C2/E
Sing praise, sing praise

Verse 2

G2
    With a mighty hand and outstretched arm, His love endures forever
C2   G
    For the life that's been reborn, His love endures for - ever
        D   C2/E   D   C2/E
Sing praise, sing praise, sing praise, sing praise

Chorus 1

    G   Em7
For - ever God is faithful, for - ever God is strong
        D   C2   G2
For - ever God is with us, for - ever for - ever

Verse 3

G2
    From the rising to the setting sun, His love endures forever
        C2   G
By the grace of God we will carry on, His love endures for - ever

Pre-Chorus

D   C2/E   D   C2/E

Sing praise, sing praise, sing praise, sing praise

Chorus 2

G   Em7

For - ever God is faithful, for - ever God is strong

D   C2

For - ever God is with us, for - ever, and ever and ever

G   Em7

For - ever God is faithful, for - ever God is strong

D   C2   G2

For - ever God is with us, for - ever, forever, for - ever

Tag

G2

Give thanks to the Lord for He is good, give thanks to the Lord for He is good

His love endures forever, His love endures forever, His love endures forever

Pre-Chorus

Chorus 3

G   Em7

For - ever You are faithful, for - ever You are strong

G/D   C2

For - ever You are with us, for - ever

G   Em7

For - ever You are faithful, for - ever You are strong

G/D   C2   G

For - ever You are with us, for - ever Ooo

God of Wonders

Words and Music by Marc Byrd
and Steve Hindalong

Key: A · Tempo: 82
CCLI Song No. 3118757

Intro (2x)
Esus / F#m7 / | D2 / / /

Verse 1
Esus F#m7   D2   Esus   F#m7   D2
     Lord of all cre - ation   of water earth and sky
Esus   F#m7   D2   Esus   F#m7   D2
     The heav - ens are Your tabernacle,   glory to the Lord on high

Chorus 1
A   Esus E   Bm7 D2
God of wonders beyond our galax - y   You are holy holy
   A   Esus E   Bm7 D2
The universe declares Your majes - ty   You are holy holy
D2   E/D   D2   E/D   D2
Lord of heaven and earth, Lord of heaven and earth

Intro (2x)

Verse 2
Esus F#m7   D2   Esus   F#m7   D2
     Early in the morning,   I will celebrate the light
Esus   F#m7   D2   Esus   F#m7   D2
     And when I stumble in the darkness,   I will call Your name by night

Chorus 1

Bridge 1
Bm7   D2   Bm7
     Hallelujah to the Lord of heaven and earth
Bm7   D2   Bm7
     Hallelujah to the Lord of heaven and earth
Bm7   D2   A
     Hallelujah to the Lord of heaven and earth

Instrumental
A / / / | Esus / E / | Bm7 D2
            Holy holy
A / / / | Esus / E   Bm7 D2
            Holy Lord

Chorus 2

A   **Esus** **E**   **Bm7** **D2**
God of wonders beyond our galax -   y   You are holy holy
    A   **Esus** **E**   **Bm7** **D2**
The universe declares Your majes -   ty   You are holy holy

Bridge 2

A   **Esus**   **Bm7**   **D2**
Precious Lord reveal Your heart to   me, Father hold me hold me
    A   **Esus**   **Bm7** **D2**
The universe declares Your majes - ty   You are holy holy

Chorus 3

A   **Esus** **E**   **Bm7** **D2**
God of wonders beyond our galax -   y   You are holy holy
    A   **Esus** **E**   **Bm7** **D2**
The universe declares Your majes -   ty   You are holy holy
        Bm7 **Dma9** | / / / / /
You are holy holy

Tag

Bm7   **D2**   **Bm7**
    Hallelujah to the Lord of heaven and earth
Bm7   **D2**   **Bm7**
    Hallelujah to the Lord of heaven and earth
Bm7   **D2**   **Bm7**
    Hallelujah to the Lord of heaven and earth
Bm7   **D2**   **A**
    Hallelujah to the Lord of heaven and earth

Esus   F#m7   D2   A   E   Bm7   E/D   Dma9

God of Wonders (CAPO 2)

Words and Music by Marc Byrd
and Steve Hindalong

Key: G · Capo: 2 (A) · Tempo: 82
CCLI Song No. 3118757

Intro (2x)
Dsus / **Em7** / | **C2** / / /

Verse 1
Dsus Em7   C2   Dsus Em7   C2
    Lord of all cre - ation   of water earth and sky
Dsus   Em7   C2   Dsus   Em7   C2
    The heav - ens are Your tabernacle,   glory to the Lord on high

Chorus 1
G   Dsus D   Am7 C2
God of wonders beyond our galax - y   You are holy holy
  G   Dsus D   Am7 C2
The universe declares Your majes - ty   You are holy holy
C2   D/C   C2   D/C   C2
Lord of heaven and earth, Lord of heaven and earth

Intro (2x)

Verse 2
Dsus Em7   C2   Dsus   Em7   C2
    Early in the morning,   I will celebrate the light
Dsus   Em7   C2   Dsus   Em7   C2
    And when I stumble in the darkness,   I will call Your name by night

Chorus 1

Bridge 1
Am7   C2   Am7
    Hallelujah to the Lord of heaven and earth
Am7   C2   Am7
    Hallelujah to the Lord of heaven and earth
Am7   C2   G
    Hallelujah to the Lord of heaven and earth

Instrumental
G / / / | **Dsus** / **D** / | **Am7 C2**
               Holy holy
G / / / | **Dsus** / **D Am7 C2**
               Holy Lord

Chorus 2

```
G                              Dsus  D       Am7  C2
God of wonders beyond our galax  -  y    You are  holy holy
  G                            Dsus  D       Am7  C2
The universe declares Your majes  -  ty    You are  holy holy
```

Bridge 2

```
G                              Dsus          Am7    C2
Precious Lord reveal Your heart to      me, Father hold me hold me
   G                           Dsus         Am7  C2
The universe declares Your majes - ty   You are  holy holy
```

Chorus 3

```
G                              Dsus  D       Am7  C2
God of wonders beyond our galax  -  y    You are  holy holy
  G                            Dsus  D       Am7  C2
The universe declares Your majes  -  ty    You are  holy holy
        Am7  Cma9 | / / / /
You are  holy  holy
```

Tag

```
Am7                 C2                 Am7
    Hallelujah to the Lord of heaven and earth
Am7                 C2                 Am7
    Hallelujah to the Lord of heaven and earth
Am7                 C2                 Am7
    Hallelujah to the Lord of heaven and earth
Am7                 C2                      G
    Hallelujah to the Lord of heaven and earth
```

Dsus   Em7   C2   G   D   Am7   D/C   Cma9

Here I Am to Worship (Light of the World)

Words and Music by
Tim Hughes

Key: F · Tempo: 76
CCLI Song No. 3266032

Intro
F / C / | Bb2 / / / | F / C / | Bb2 / / /

Verse 1
F   C   Gm7   F   C   Bb2
Light of the world You stepped down into darkness, opened my eyes let me see
F   C   Gm7   F   C   Bb2
Beauty that made this heart adore You, hope of a life spent with You

Chorus
          F   C/E   F/A   Bb2
Here I am to worship here I am to bow down, here I am to say that You're my God
        F   C/E   F/A   Bb2
You're altogether lovely altogether worthy, altogether wonderful to me

Verse 2
F   C   Gm7   F   C   Bb2
King of all days oh so highly exalted, glorious in heaven above
F   C   Gm7   F   C   Bb2
Humbly You came to the earth You created, all for love's sake became poor

Chorus

Bridge (2x)
  C/E   F/A   Bb2   C/E   F/A   Bb2
I'll never know how much it cost to see my sin up - on that cross

Chorus > **Bridge** > **Chorus (3x)**

Ending
(Bb2) / / / | / / Csus4 / | Bb2 / / / | / / Csus4 /
Bb2 / / / | / / Csus4 / | Bb2

F   C   Bb2   Gm7   C/E   F/A   Csus4

Here I Am to Worship (Light of the World)
(CAPO 1)

Words and Music by
Tim Hughes

Key: E · Capo: 1 (F) · Tempo: 76
CCLI Song No. 3266032

Intro
E / B / | A2 / / / | E / B / | A2 / / /

Verse 1
E   B   F#m7   E   B   A2
Light of the world You stepped down into darkness, opened my eyes let me see
E   B   F#m7   E   B   A2
Beauty that made this heart adore You, hope of a life spent with You

Chorus
E   B/D#   E/G#   A2
Here I am to worship here I am to bow down, here I am to say that You're my God
E   B/D#   E/G#   A2
You're altogether lovely altogether worthy, altogether wonderful to me

Verse 2
E   B   F#m7 E   B   A2
King of all days oh so highly exalted, glorious in heaven above
E   B   F#m7   E   B   A2
Humbly You came to the earth You created, all for love's sake became poor

Chorus

Bridge (2x)
B/D# E/G#   A2   B/D#   E/G#   A2
I'll never know how much it cost to see my sin up - on that cross

Chorus > Bridge > Chorus (3x)

Ending
(A2) / / / | / / Bsus4 / | A2 / / / | / / Bsus4 /
A2 / / / | / / Bsus4 / | A2

  E   B   A2   F#m7   B/D#   E/G# Bsus4

Holy Is the Lord

Words and Music by Chris Tomlin
and Louie Giglio

Key: A · Tempo: 84
CCLI Song No. 4158039

Intro
A5 / D2 / | Esus4 / / / | F#m7 / D2 / | Esus4 / / /

Verse
A5   D2   Esus4   F#m7   D2   Esus4
   We stand and lift up our hands, for the joy of the Lord is our strength
A5   D2   Esus4   F#m7   D2   Esus4
   We bow down and worship Him now, how great how awesome is   He
                B   D2   B   D2
And together we sing,   everyone sing

Chorus 1
        A/C# D2   Esus4   F#m7 D2   Esus4
Holy is the Lord God Al - mighty, the earth is filled with His glory
        A/C# D2   Esus4   F#m7 D2   Esus4
Holy is the Lord God Al - mighty, the earth is filled with His glory
   F#m7 D2   Esus4
The earth is filled with His glory

Verse > **Chorus 1**

Bridge
  A   E/G#   G6   D
It is rising up all around, it's the anthem of the Lord's renown
  A   E/G#   G6   D
It's rising up all around, it's the anthem of the Lord's renown
               B   D2   B   D2
And together we sing,   every - one sing

Chorus 1

Instrumental (4x)
F#m7 / A2/G# - A2 | E / / /

Chorus 2
       A/C# D2   Esus4   A/C# D2   Esus4
Holy is the Lord God Al - mighty, the earth is filled with His glory
       A/C# D2   Esus4   A/C# D2   Esus4
Holy is the Lord God Al - mighty, the earth is filled with His glory

Tag
Holy is the Lord God Almighty, the earth is filled with His glory
                 A/C#   D2   Esus4
Holy is the Lord God Almighty, the earth is filled with His glory
  A/C# D2   Esus4 F#m7 D2   E A2
The earth is filled with His glory, the earth is filled with His glory

Holy Is the Lord (CAPO 2)

· ·

Words and Music by Chris Tomlin
and Louie Giglio

Key: G · Capo: 2 (A) · Tempo: 84
CCLI Song No. 4158039

Intro
G5 / C2 / / | Dsus4 / / / | Em7 / C2 / / | Dsus4 / / /

Verse
G5   C2   Dsus4   Em7   C2   Dsus4
    We stand and lift up our hands, for the joy of the Lord is our strength
G5   C2   Dsus4   Em7   C2   Dsus4
    We bow down and worship Him now, how great how awesome is   He
                    A   C2   A   C2
And together we sing,   everyone sing

Chorus 1
          G/B C2   Dsus4   Em7   C2   Dsus4
Holy is the Lord God Al - mighty, the earth is filled with His glory
          G/B C2   Dsus4   Em7   C2   Dsus4
Holy is the Lord God Al - mighty, the earth is filled with His glory
    Em7   C2   Dsus4
The earth is filled with His glory

Verse > Chorus 1

Bridge
  G   D/F#   F6   C
It is rising up   all   around, it's the anthem of the Lord's renown
  G   D/F#   F6   C
It's rising up   all   around, it's the anthem of the Lord's renown
                 A   C2   A   C2
And together we sing,   every - one sing

Chorus 1

Instrumental (4x)
Em7 / G2/F# - G2 | D / / /

Chorus 2

      G/B C2   **Dsus4**   **G/B**   **C2**   **Dsus4**
Holy is the Lord God Al - mighty, the earth is filled with His glory
      G/B C2   **Dsus4**   **G/B**   **C2**   **Dsus4**
Holy is the Lord God Al - mighty, the earth is filled with His glory

Tag

Holy is the Lord God Almighty, the earth is filled with His glory
                       G/B   **C2**   **Dsus4**
Holy is the Lord God Almighty, the earth is filled with His glory
   G/B   **C2**   **Dsus4 Em7**   **C2**   **D**   **G2**
The earth is filled with His glory, the earth is filled with His glory

G5   C2   Em7   A   G/B   G   D/F#   F6   C   G2/F#   G2   D

In Christ Alone

Words and Music by Keith Getty
and Stuart Townend

Key: D · Tempo: 62
CCLI Song No. 3350395

Intro (2x)
Am7 / / | Em7 / / | D / G/D | D / /

Verse 1

```
  G/D      D      G      A     D/F#      G   D/F# Em7   G/A      D
In Christ a - lone my hope is found,  He is my light  my   strength    my song
  G        D      G      A      D/F#          G   D/F# Em7   G/A      D
This corner - stone this solid ground, firm through the fier - cest  drought     and storm
     D/F#      G         Bm7     A        D/F#    G          Bm       A
What heights of love what depths of peace, when fears are stilled when strivings cease
  G        D      G      A   D/F#      G   D/F# Em7  G/A  D    / G/D | D
My Comfort - er my All in all, here in the love   of   Christ    I stand
```

Verse 2

```
  G/D      D      G      A     D/F#      G   D/F# Em7  G/A        D
In Christ a - lone who took on flesh, fullness of God   in   help    - less babe
  G        D      G      A      D/F#          G   D/F# Em7   G/A      D
This gift of love and righteous - ness, scorned by the ones   He   came     to save
     D/F#      G         Bm7  A       D/F#    G          Bm       A
Till  on  that cross as Jesus died, the wrath of God was satis - fied
  G        D      G      A   D/F#      G   D/F# Em7  G/A  D
For every sin on Him was laid, here in the death   of   Christ    I live
```

Instrumental 1 (2x)
Am7 / / | Em7 / / | D / G/D | D / /

Verse 3

```
     G/D    D      G    A   D/F#    G     D/F# Em7 G/A      D
There  in  the ground His body lay, light of the world     by dark  -  ness slain
     G/D    D    G    A   D/F#      G     D/F# Em7 G/A    D
Then bursting forth in glorious day,  up  from the grave  He  rose     a - gain
     D/F#   G        Bm7  A     D/F#    G    Bm      A
And  as  He stands in victo - ry, sin's curse has lost its grip on me
     G    D     G    A   D/F#        G    D/F# Em7 G/A  D
For I am His and He is mine, bought with the pre - cious blood    of Christ
```

Instrumental 2

```
Am7 / / |  Em7 / / |  D / G/D |  D / /
Am7 / / |  Em7 / / |  D / G/D |  D / /
Am7 / / |  Em7 / / |  D / G/D |  D / /
Am7 / / |  Em7 / / |  D / / / |  / /
```

Verse 4

```
     G     D    G    A    D/F#     G    D/F# Em7 G/A   D
No guilt in life no fear in death, this is the power  of   Christ    in me
     G/D   D    G    A    D/F#       G    D/F# Em7 G/A    D
From life's first cry to final breath, Jesus com - mands  my   des  -  ti - ny
     D/F#  G     Bm7   A      D/F# G      Bm7    A
No power of hell no scheme of man, can  ever  pluck me from His hand
     G    D    G    A    D/F#      G    D/F# Em7 G/A  D
Till He re - turns or calls me home, here in the power  of   Christ     I'll stand
```

Instrumental 1 (2x)

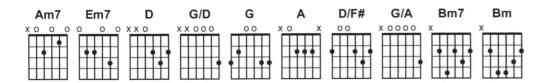

Mighty to Save

Words and Music by Ben Fielding
and Reuben Morgan

Key: A · Tempo: 72
CCLI Song No. 4591782

Intro (3x)

A / / / / | / / / /

Instrumental 1 (2x)

D / / / / | A / / / / | F#m7 / / / / | E / / /

Verse 1

D   A   F#m7   E
  Everyone needs com - passion, a love that's never failing, let mercy fall on me
D   A   F#m7   E
  Everyone needs for - giveness, the kindness of a Saviour, the hope of nations
D / E / | D / E /

Chorus

A   E
Saviour He can move the mountains
        D   A   F#m   E
My God is mighty to save, He is mighty to save
     A   E
For - ever Author of sal - vation
        D   A   F#m   E
He rose and conquered the grave, Jesus conquered the grave

Instrumental 1

Verse 2

D   A   F#m7   E
  So take me as You find me, all my fears and failures, fill my life again
D   A   F#m7   E
  I give my life to follow everything I be - lieve in, now I surrender
D / E / | D / E /

Chorus (2x)

Instrumental 2
D / A / | E / / F#m | D / A / | E / / F#m

Bridge (2x)
```
D                        A              E       F#m
  Shine Your light and   let the whole world see, we're singing
D           A         E    F#m
  For the glory   of the risen King, Jesus
D                        A              E       F#m
  Shine Your light and   let the whole world see, we're singing
D           A         E
  For the glory   of the risen King
```

Chorus (2x) > Bridge (3x)

Mighty to Save (CAPO 2)

Words and Music by Ben Fielding
and Reuben Morgan

Key: G · Capo: 2 (A) · Tempo: 72
CCLI Song No. 4591782

Intro (3x)
G / / / / | / / / /

Instrumental 1 (2x)
C / / / / | G / / / / | Em7 / / / / | D / / /

Verse 1
C   G   Em7   D
   Everyone needs com - passion, a love that's never failing, let mercy fall on me
C   G   Em7   D
   Everyone needs for - giveness, the kindness of a Saviour, the hope of nations
C / D / | C / D /

Chorus
G   D
Saviour He can move the mountains
            C   G   Em   D
My God is mighty to save, He is mighty to save
       G   D
For - ever Author of sal - vation
            C   G   Em   D
He rose and conquered the grave, Jesus conquered the grave

Instrumental 1

Verse 2
C   G   Em7   D
   So take me as You find me, all my fears and failures, fill my life again
C   G   Em7   D
   I give my life to follow, everything I be - lieve in, now I surrender
C / D / | C / D /

Chorus (2x)

Instrumental 2
C / G / | D / / Em | C / G / | D / / Em

Bridge (2x)
```
C                       G                   D           Em
  Shine Your light and    let the whole world see, we're singing
C         G             D      Em
  For the glory    of the risen King, Jesus
C                       G                   D           Em
  Shine Your light and    let the whole world see, we're singing
C         G             D
  For the glory    of the risen King
```


Chorus (2x) > Bridge (3x)

Sing to the King

Words and Music by Billy James Foote

Key: F · Tempo: 122
CCLI Song No. 4010902

Intro (2x)
F / / / / | F2 / / / / | Fsus / / / | F / / /

Verse 1
F   C/F   Bb/F   F   C/F   Bb/F   F
Sing to the King who is coming to reign, glory to Jesus the Lamb that was slain
F   C/E   Bb/D   F/A   Dm7   C   Bb   F
Life and sal - vation His empire shall bring, joy to the nations when Jesus is King

Chorus 1
  F   Gm7   Bb   F | Eb2 - Bb /
So come let us sing a song, a song declaring we belong to Jesus, He is all we need
F   Gm7   Bb   C   F
Lift up a heart of praise, sing now with voices raised to Jesus,   sing to the King

Intro (2x)

Verse 2
F   C/F   Bb/F   F   C/F   Bb/F   F
For His re - turning we watch and we pray, we will be ready the dawn of that day
F   C/E   Bb/D   F/A   Dm7   C   Bb   F
We'll join in singing with all   the re - deemed, Satan is vanquished and Jesus is King

Chorus 1 > Intro (2x) > Verse 2

Chorus 2
  F   Gm7   Bb   F | Eb2 - Bb/D - Bb
So come let us sing a song, a song declaring we belong to Jesus, He is all we need
F   Gm7   Bb   C   F | Eb2 - Bb /
Lift up a heart of praise, sing now with voices raised to Jesus,   sing to the King

Chorus 3
  F   Gm7   Bb   F | Eb2 - Bb/D - Bb
So come let us sing a song, a song declaring we belong to Jesus, He is all we need
F   Gm7   Bb   C   F
Lift up a heart of praise, sing now with voices raised to Jesus, sing to the King

End
F / / / / | F2 / / / / | Fsus / / / | F / / /
F / / / / | F2 / / / / | Fsus / / / / | F / / /

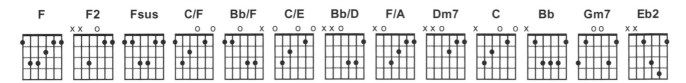

Sing to the King (CAPO 1)

Key: E · Capo: 1 (F) · Tempo: 122
CCLI Song No. 4010902

Words and Music by Billy James Foote

Intro (2x)
E / / / | E2 / / / | Esus / / / | E / / /

Verse 1
E B/E A/E E   B/E A/E   E
Sing to the King who is coming to reign, glory to Jesus the Lamb that was slain
E B/D# A/C# E/G# C#m7 B   A   E
Life and sal - vation His empire shall bring, joy to the nations when Jesus is King

Chorus 1
 E   F#m7   A   E | D2 - A /
So come let us sing a song, a song declaring we belong to Jesus, He is all we need
E   F#m7   A B   E
Lift up a heart of praise, sing now with voices raised to Jesus, sing to the King

Intro (2x)

Verse 2
E B/E A/E E   B/E A/E   E
For His re - turning we watch and we pray, we will be ready the dawn of that day
E B/D# A/C# E/G# C#m7 B   A   E
We'll join in singing with all the re - deemed, Satan is vanquished and Jesus is King

Chorus 1 > Intro (2x) > Verse 2

Chorus 2
 E   F#m7   A   E | D2 - A/C# - A
So come let us sing a song, a song declaring we belong to Jesus, He is all we need
E   F#m7   A B   E | D2 - A /
Lift up a heart of praise, sing now with voices raised to Jesus, sing to the King

Chorus 3
 E   F#m7   A   E | D2 - A/C# - A
So come let us sing a song, a song declaring we belong to Jesus, He is all we need
E   F#m7   A B   E
Lift up a heart of praise, sing now with voices raised to Jesus, sing to the King

End
E / / / | E2 / / / | Esus / / / | E / / /
E / / / | E2 / / / | Esus / / / | E / / /

Chord diagrams: E, E2, Esus, B/E, A/E, B/D#, A/C#, E/G#, C#m7, B, A, F#m7, D2

Your Name

Words and Music by Paul Baloche
and Glenn Packiam

Key: Bb · Tempo: 80
CCLI Song No. 4611679

Intro (2x)
Bb/D / Ebma9 / | F/A / Bb5 /

Verse 1

| Bb/D Eb2   F   Bb5 Bb/D   Eb2 F   Bb5 |
As morning dawns and evening fades You in - spire songs of praise
| Bb/D   Eb2   F   Gm7   Eb2 F   Bb5 |
That rise from earth to touch Your heart and glori - fy Your name

Chorus 1

| Dm7 Gm7   Bb   Eb2 |
Your Name   is a strong and mighty tower
| F   Gm7   Bb   Eb2 |
Your Name   is a shelter like no other
| F   Gm7   Bb   Eb2 |
Your Name,   let the nations sing it louder
| Bb/D   Eb2   Fsus F   Bb/D |
'Cause nothing has the power to save   but Your Name

Intro

Verse 2

| Bb/D Eb2   F   Bb5 Bb/D   Eb2   F   Bb5 |
Jesus in Your Name we pray, come and fill our hearts to - day
| Bb/D   Eb2   F   Gm7   Eb2 F   Bb5 |
Lord give us strength to live for You and glori - fy Your Name

Chorus 2

```
        Dm7  Gm7     Bb                    Eb2
Your  Name             is a strong and mighty tower
        F    Gm7     Bb                Eb2
Your Name              is a shelter like no other
        F    Gm7        Bb               Eb2
Your Name,           let the nations sing it louder
     Bb/D          Eb2      Fsus  F         Gm
'Cause nothing has the power to  save    but Your Name
```

Instrumental

```
(Gm) / / / |  F / / / |  Csus / C / | / / / / |
Gm7 / / / |  F / / / |  Csus / C / |  Eb2 / / / | / / /
```

Chorus 3

```
        F    Gm7     Bb                    Eb2
Your Name              is a strong and mighty tower
        F    Gm7     Bb                Eb2
Your Name              is a shelter like no other
        F    Gm7        Bb               Eb2
Your Name,           let the nations sing it louder
     Bb/D          Eb2      Fsus  F
'Cause nothing has the power to  save    but
```

Chorus 1

Tag (2x)

```
(Bb/D) / Eb2 / |  F / Bb5 / |
Bb/D / Eb2 / |  F / Bb / |  F / Bb /
```

Your Name (CAPO 3)

· ·

Words and Music by Paul Baloche
and Glenn Packiam

Key: G · Capo: 3 (Bb) · Tempo: 80
CCLI Song No. 4611679

Intro (2x)
G/B / Cma9 / | D/F# / G5 /

Verse 1
| G/B | C2 | D | G5 | G/B | C2 | D | G5 |
As morning dawns and evening fades You in - spire songs of praise
| G/B | C2 | D | Em7 | C2 | D | G5 |
That rise from earth to touch Your heart and glori - fy Your name

Chorus 1
| Bm7 Em7 | G | | C2 |
Your Name   is a strong and mighty tower
| D | Em7 | G | | C2 |
Your Name   is a shelter like no other
| D | Em7 | G | | C2 |
Your Name,   let the nations sing it louder
| G/B | C2 | Dsus D | G/B |
'Cause nothing has the power to save   but Your Name

Intro

Verse 2
| G/B | C2 | D | G5 | G/B | C2 | D | G5 |
Jesus in Your Name we pray, come and fill our hearts to - day
| G/B | C2 | D | Em7 | C2 | D | G5 |
Lord give us strength to live for You and glori - fy Your Name

Chorus 2

```
        Bm7  Em7    G                  C2
Your  Name          is a strong and mighty tower
          D    Em7    G             C2
Your Name          is a shelter like no other
          D    Em7      G            C2
Your Name,         let the nations sing it louder
       G/B           C2        Dsus  D        Em
'Cause nothing has the power to  save    but Your Name
```

Instrumental

```
(Em) / / / |  D / / / |  Asus / A / | / / / / |
Em7 / / / |  D / / / |  Asus / A / |  C2 / / / | / / /
```

Chorus 3

```
          D    Em7    G                  C2
Your Name          is a strong and mighty tower
          D    Em7    G             C2
Your Name          is a shelter like no other
          D    Em7      G            C2
Your Name,         let the nations sing it louder
       G/B           C2        Dsus  D
'Cause nothing has the power to  save    but
```

Chorus 1

Tag (2x)

```
(G/B) / C2 / |  D / G5 / |
G/B / C2 / |  D / G / |  D / G /
```

Amazing Grace
(My Chains Are Gone)

Rhythm Chart

Words by John Newton
Traditional American Melody
Additional Words and Music by Chris Tomlin and Louie Giglio
Arranged by Dan Galbraith

Blessed Be Your Name

Words and Music by Matt Redman and Beth Redman
Arranged by Dan Galbraith and Shane Ohlson

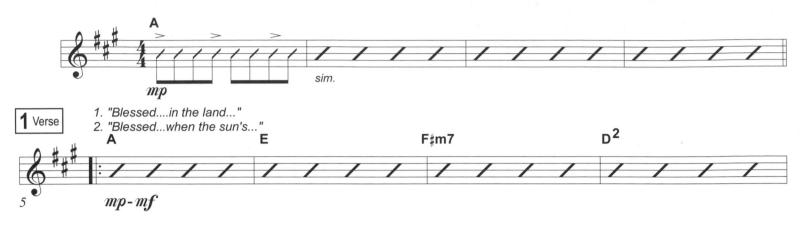

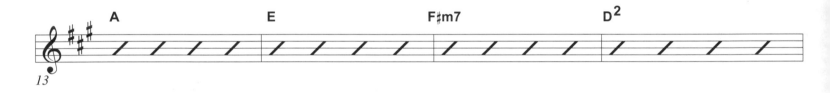

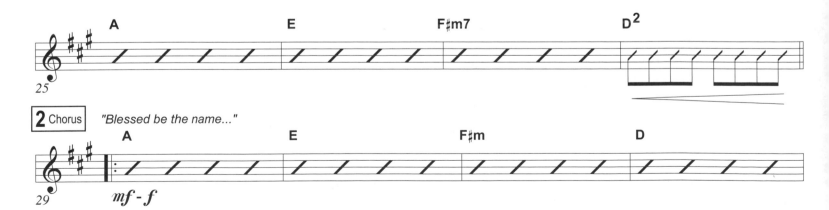

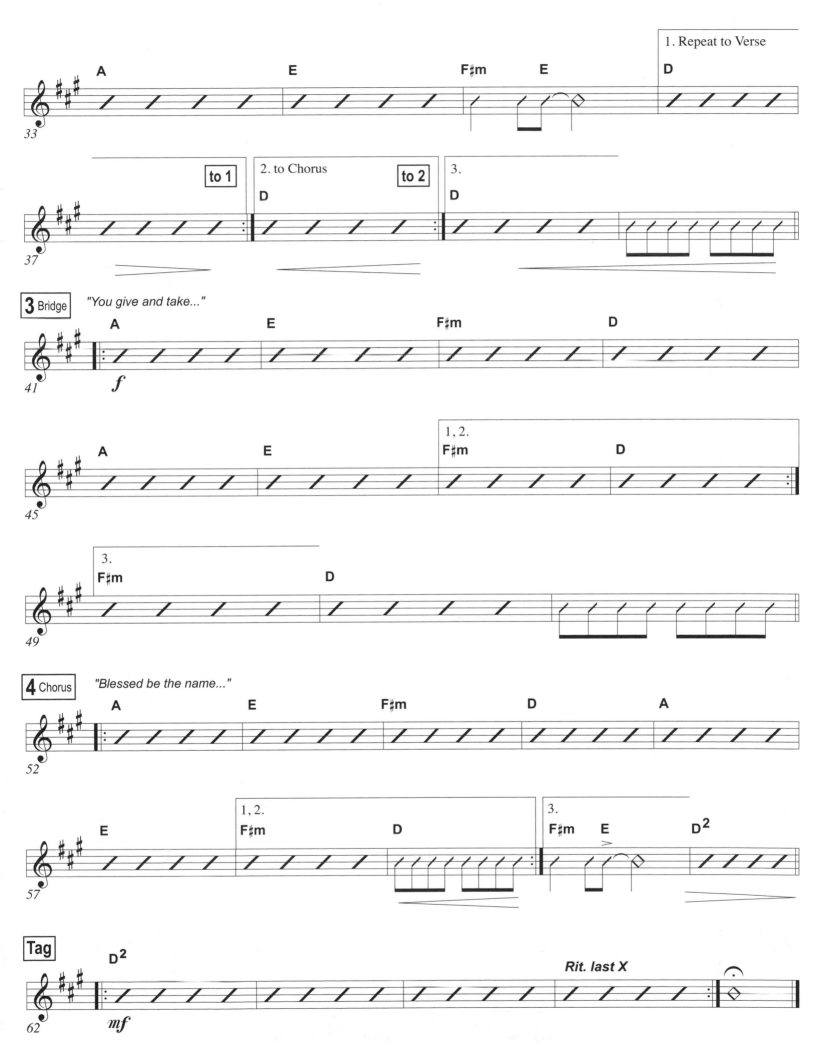

Forever

Rhythm Chart

Words and Music by Chris Tomlin
Arranged by Dan Galbraith

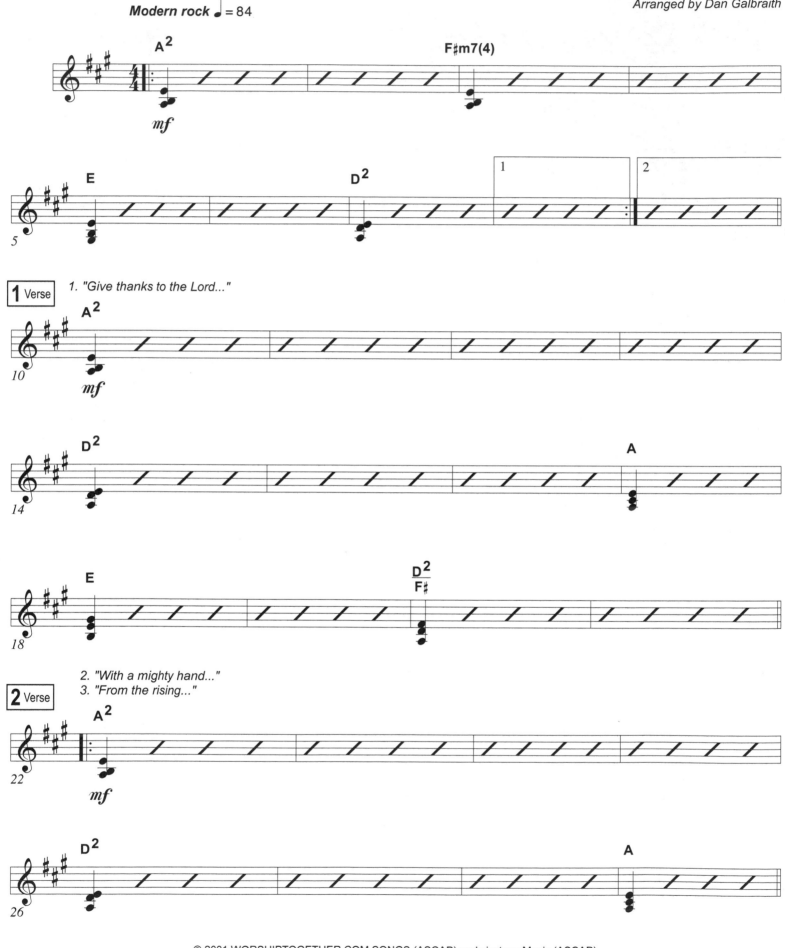

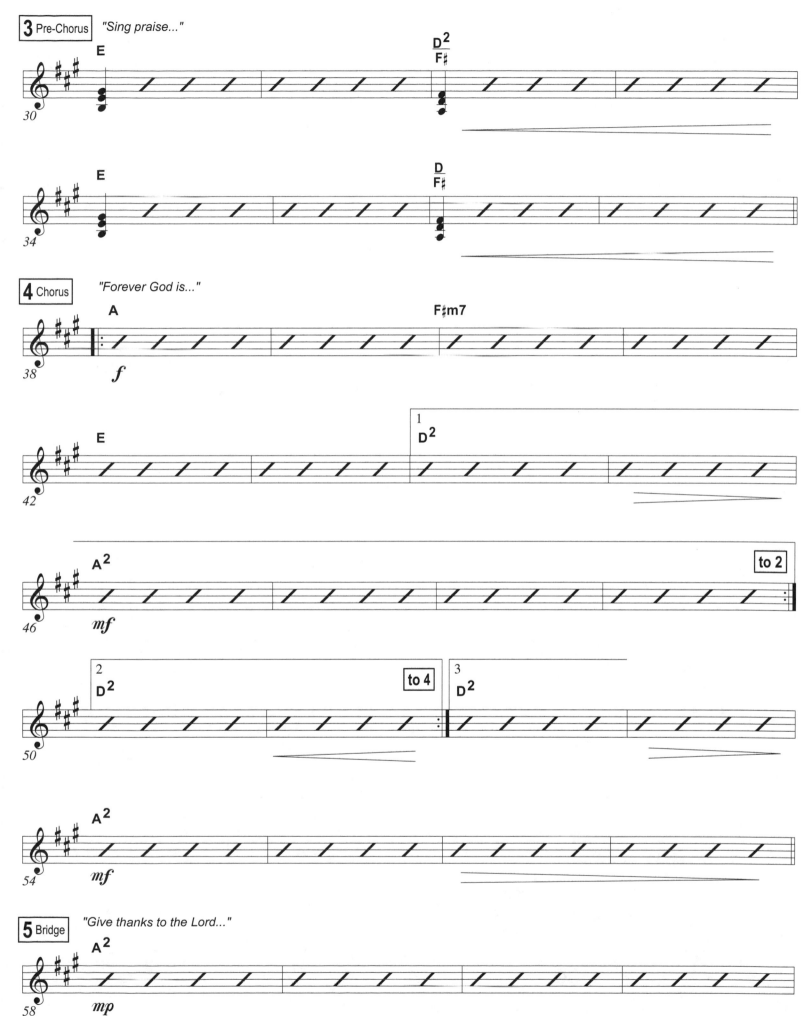

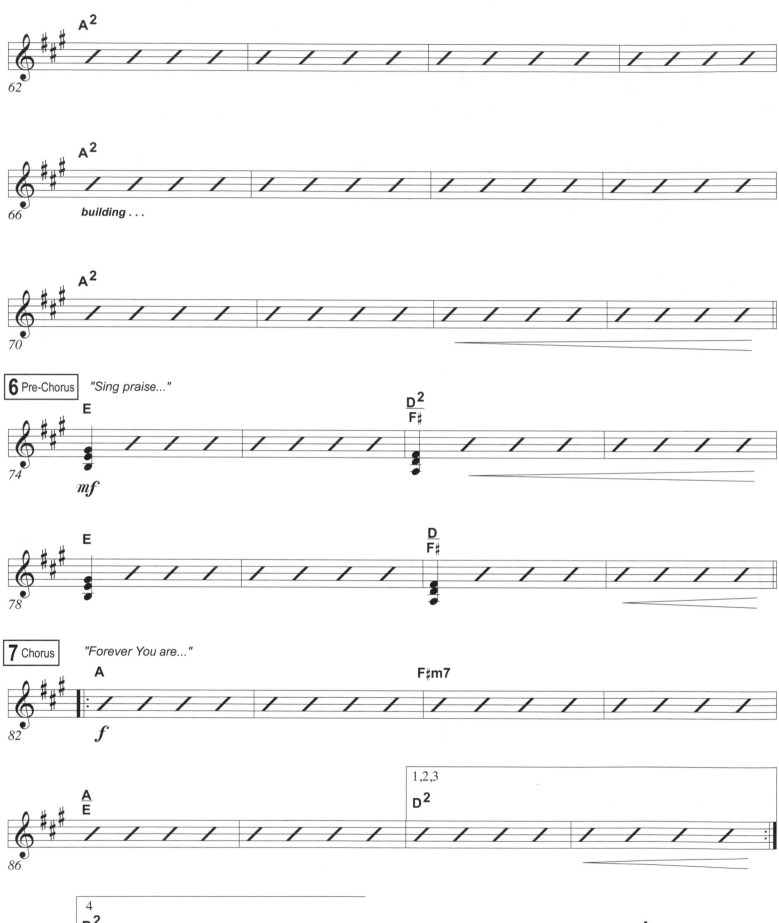

In Christ Alone

Rhythm Chart

Words and Music by Keith Getty and Stuart Townend
Arranged by Dan Galbraith

1. "In Christ alone my hope is found..."
2. "In Christ alone, Who took on flesh..."

God of Wonders

Words and Music by Marc Byrd and Steve Hindalong
Arranged by Dan Galbraith and Dave Iula

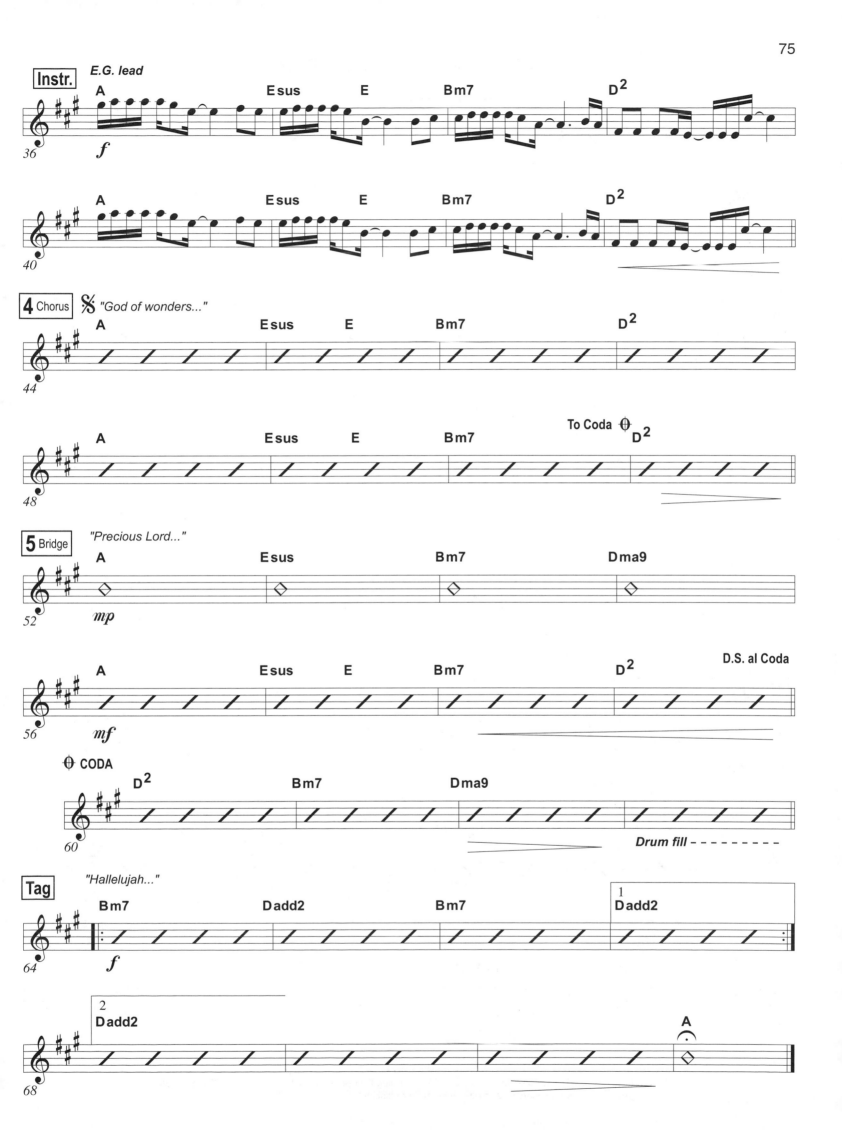

Here I Am to Worship
(Light of the World)

Rhythm Chart

Words and Music by Tim Hughes
Arranged by Dan Galbraith

Holy Is the Lord

Words and Music by Chris Tomlin and Louie Giglio
Arranged by Dan Galbraith

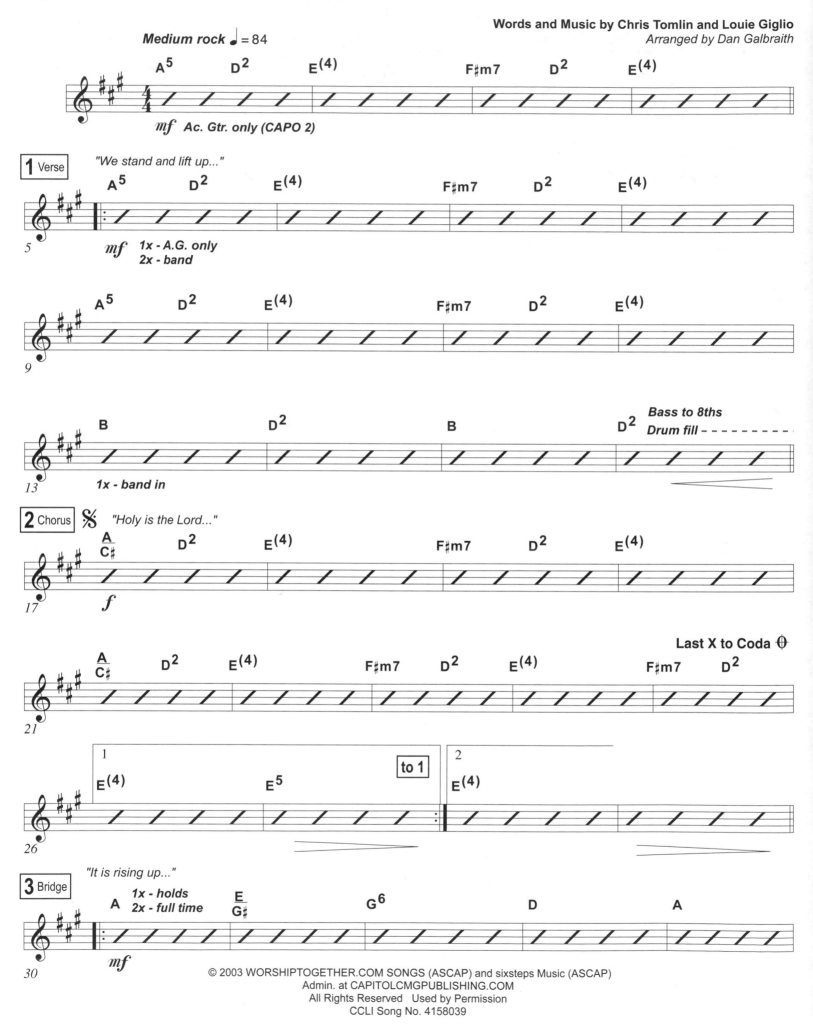

Mighty to Save

Words and Music by Ben Fielding and Reuben Morgan
Arranged by Dan Galbraith

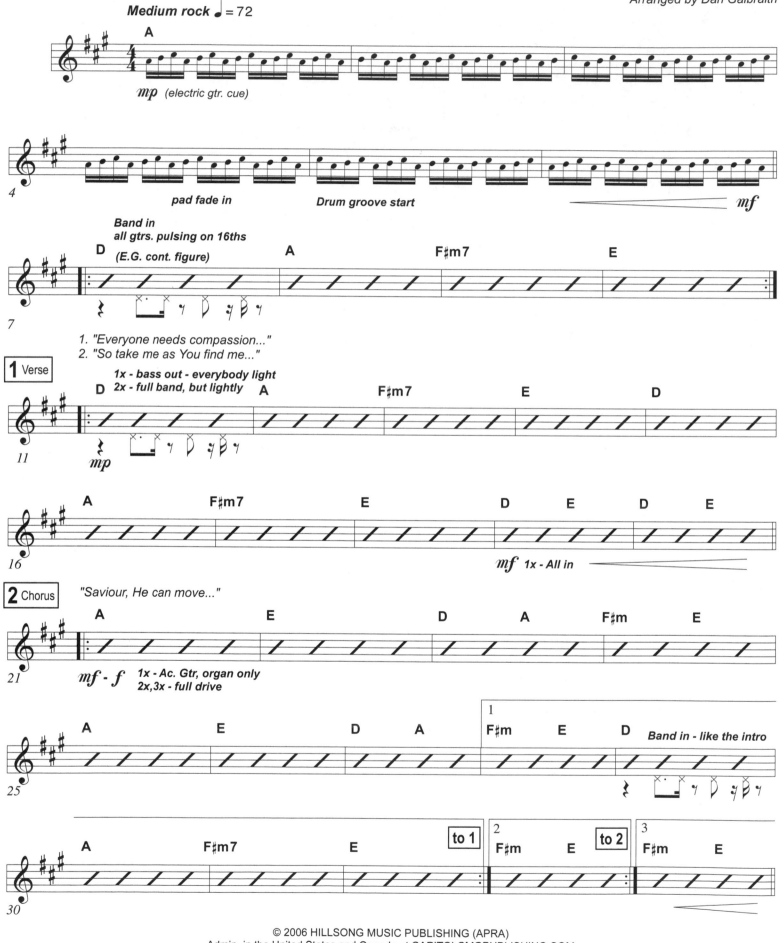

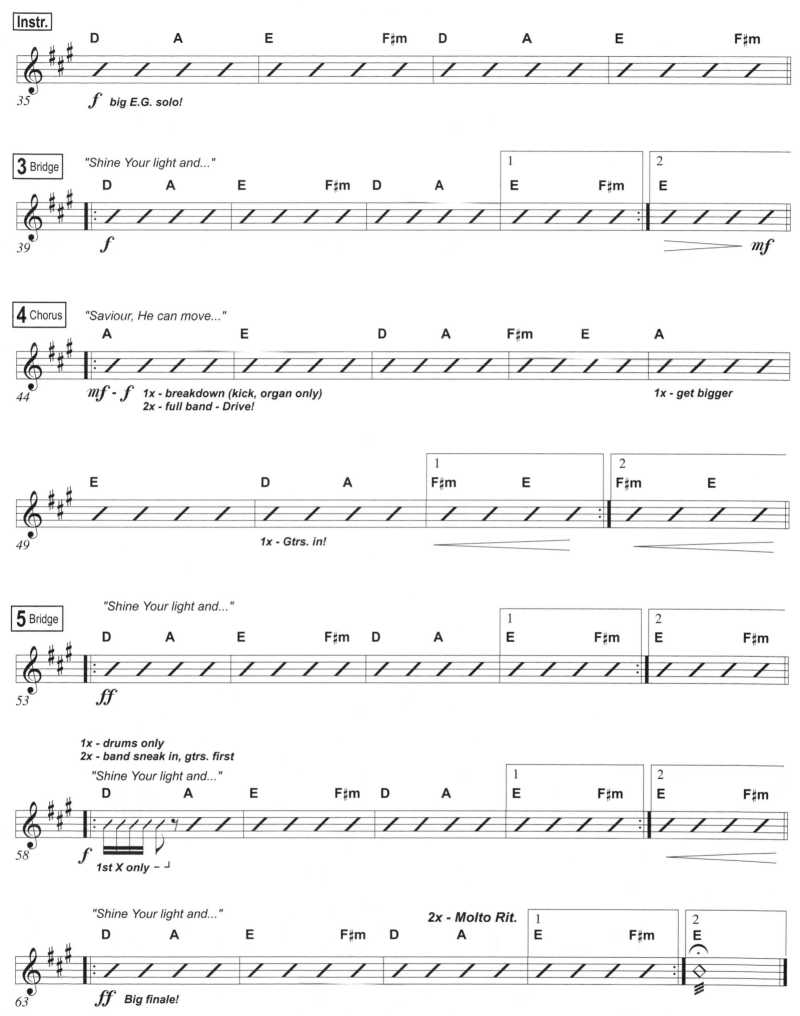

Sing to the King

Words and Music by Billy James Foote
Arranged by Dan Galbraith

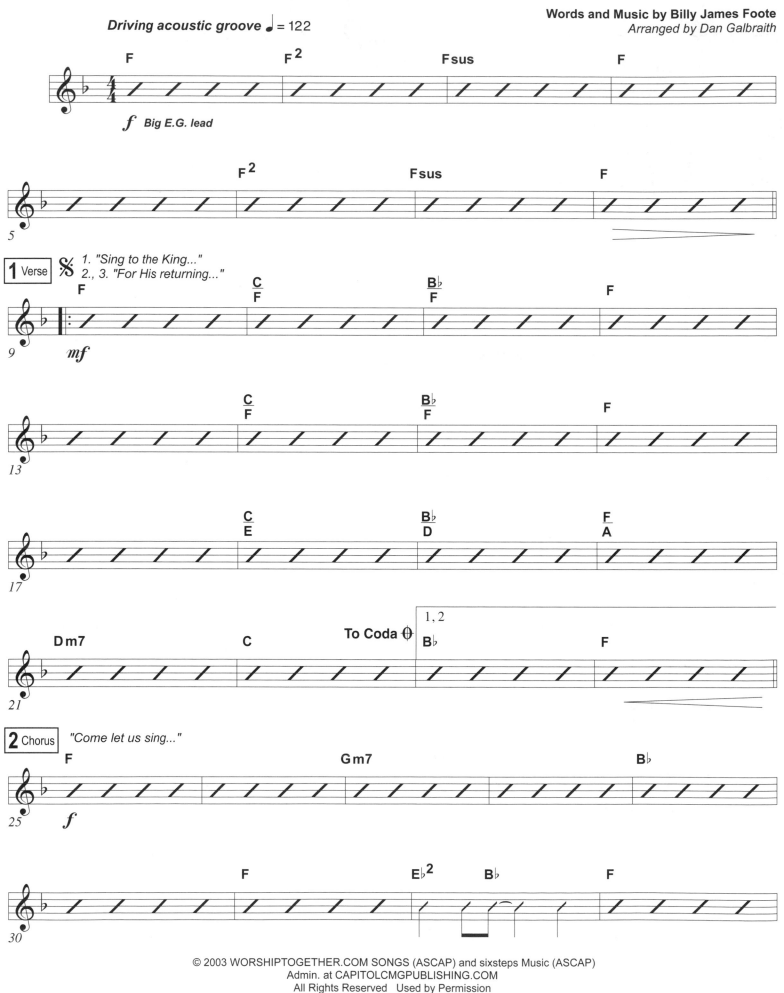

Your Name

Words and Music by Paul Baloche and Glenn Packiam
Arranged by Dan Galbraith

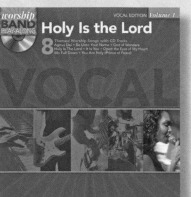

Worship Band Play-Along

The **Worship Band Play-Along** series is a flexible tool for worship leaders and bands. Each volume offers five separate, correlated book/CD packs: Guitar, Keyboard, Bass, Drumset, and Vocal. Bands can use the printed music and chord charts to play live together, and members can rehearse at home with the CD tracks. Worship leaders without a band can play/sing along with the CD for a fuller sound. The eight songs in each volume follow a similar theme for easy set selection, and the straightforward arrangements are perfect for bands of any level.

1. Holy Is the Lord

Includes: Agnus Dei • Be Unto Your Name • God of Wonders • Holy Is the Lord • It Is You • Open the Eyes of My Heart • We Fall Down • You Are Holy (Prince of Peace).

08740302	Vocal	$12.95
08740333	Keyboard	$12.95
08740334	Guitar	$12.95
08740335	Bass	$12.95
08740336	Drumset	$12.95

2. Here I Am to Worship

Includes: Come, Now Is the Time to Worship • Give Us Clean Hands • Hear Our Praises • Here I Am to Worship • I Give You My Heart • Let Everything That Has Breath • You Alone • You're Worthy of My Praise.

08740337	Vocal	$12.95
08740338	Keyboard	$12.95
08740409	Guitar	$12.95
08740441	Bass	$12.95
08740444	Drumset	$12.95

3. How Great Is Our God

Includes: Above All • Beautiful Savior (All My Days) • Days of Elijah • How Great Is Our God • Let My Words Be Few (I'll Stand in Awe of You) • No One Like You • Wonderful Maker • Yesterday, Today and Forever.

08740540	Vocal	$12.95
08740571	Keyboard	$12.95
08740572	Guitar	$12.95
08740608	Bass	$12.95
08740635	Drumset	$12.95

4. He Is Exalted

Includes: Beautiful One • God of All • He Is Exalted • In Christ Alone • Lord Most High • Lord, Reign in Me • We Want to See Jesus Lifted High • Worthy Is the Lamb.

08740646	Vocal	$12.99
08740651	Keyboard	$12.99
08740712	Guitar	$12.99
08740741	Bass	$12.99
08745665	Drumset	$12.99

5. Joy to the World

Angels We Have Heard on High • Away in a Manger • Hark! the Herald Angels Sing • Joy to the World • O Come, All Ye Faithful (Adeste Fideles) • O Come, O Come, Emmanuel • Silent Night • What Child Is This?.

08749919	Vocal	$12.99
08749921	Guitar	$12.99
08749923	Drumset	$12.99

For More Information, See Your Local Music Dealer, Or Write To:

HAL•LEONARD® CORPORATION
7777 W. Bluemound Rd. P.O. Box 13819 Milwaukee, WI 53213

www.halleonard.com

Prices, contents, and availability
subject to change without notice.

The Best
PRAISE & WORSHIP
Songbooks for Piano

Above All
THE PHILLIP KEVEREN SERIES
15 beautiful praise song piano solo arrangements by Phillip Keveren. Includes: Above All • Agnus Dei • Breathe • Draw Me Close • He Is Exalted • I Stand in Awe • Step by Step • We Fall Down • You Are My King (Amazing Love) • and more.
00311024 Piano Solo.................................$11.95

The Best Praise & Worship Songs Ever
80 all-time favorites: Awesome God • Breathe • Days of Elijah • Here I Am to Worship • I Could Sing of Your Love Forever • Open the Eyes of My Heart • Shout to the Lord • We Bow Down • dozens more.
00311057 P/V/G $22.99

More of the Best Praise & Worship Songs Ever
76 more contemporary worship favorites, including: Beautiful One • Everlasting God • Friend of God • How Great Is Our God • In Christ Alone • Let It Rise • Mighty to Save • Your Grace Is Enough • more.
00311800 P/V/G $24.99

The Big Book of Praise & Worship
Over 50 worship favorites are presented in this popular "Big Book" series collection. Includes: Always • Cornerstone • Forever Reign • I Will Follow • Jesus Paid It All • Lord, I Need You • Mighty to Save • Our God • Stronger • 10,000 Reasons (Bless the Lord) • This Is Amazing Grace • and more.
00140795 P/V/G $22.99

Contemporary Worship Duets
arr. Bill Wolaver
Contains 8 powerful songs carefully arranged by Bill Wolaver as duets for intermediate-level players: Agnus Dei • Be unto Your Name • He Is Exalted • Here I Am to Worship • I Will Rise • The Potter's Hand • Revelation Song • Your Name.
00290593 Piano Duets $10.99

51 Must-Have Modern Worship Hits
A great collection of 51 of today's most popular worship songs, including: Amazed • Better Is One Day • Everyday • Forever • God of Wonders • He Reigns • How Great Is Our God • Offering • Sing to the King • You Are Good • and more.
00311428 P/V/G $22.99

Hillsong Worship Favorites
12 powerful worship songs arranged for piano solo: At the Cross • Came to My Rescue • Desert Song • Forever Reign • Holy Spirit Rain Down • None but Jesus • The Potter's Hand • The Stand • Stronger • and more.
00312522 Piano Solo.................................$12.99

The Best of Passion
Over 40 worship favorites featuring the talents of David Crowder, Matt Redman, Chris Tomlin, and others. Songs include: Always • Awakening • Blessed Be Your Name • Jesus Paid It All • My Heart Is Yours • Our God • 10,000 Reasons (Bless the Lord) • and more.
00101888 P/V/G $19.99

Praise & Worship Duets
THE PHILLIP KEVEREN SERIES
8 worshipful duets by Phillip Keveren: As the Deer • Awesome God • Give Thanks • Great Is the Lord • Lord, I Lift Your Name on High • Shout to the Lord • There Is a Redeemer • We Fall Down.
00311203 Piano Duet................................ $11.95

Shout to the Lord!
THE PHILLIP KEVEREN SERIES
14 favorite praise songs, including: As the Deer • El Shaddai • Give Thanks • Great Is the Lord • How Beautiful • More Precious Than Silver • Oh Lord, You're Beautiful • A Shield About Me • Shine, Jesus, Shine • Shout to the Lord • Thy Word • and more.
00310699 Piano Solo $12.95

The Chris Tomlin Collection – 2nd Edition
15 songs from one of the leading artists and composers in Contemporary Christian music, including the favorites: Amazing Grace (My Chains Are Gone) • Holy Is the Lord • How Can I Keep from Singing • How Great Is Our God • Jesus Messiah • Our God • We Fall Down • and more.
00306951 P/V/G $16.99

Top Worship Downloads
20 of today's chart-topping Christian hits, including: Cornerstone • Forever Reign • Great I Am • Here for You • Lord, I Need You • My God • Never Once • One Thing Remains (Your Love Never Fails) • Your Great Name • and more.
00120870 P/V/G $16.99

Worship Together Piano Solo Favorites
A dozen great worship songs tastefully arranged for intermediate piano solo. Includes: Amazing Grace (My Chains Are Gone) • Beautiful Savior (All My Days) • Facedown • The Heart of Worship • How Great Is Our God • and more.
00311477 Piano Solo.................................$12.95

Worship Without Words
arr. Ken Medema
The highly creative Ken Medema has arranged 13 worship songs and classic hymns, perfect for blended worship. Includes: As the Deer • I Could Sing of Your Love Forever • Open the Eyes of My Heart • You Are My All in All • and more.
00311229 Piano Solo.................................$12.95

7777 W. BLUEMOUND RD. P.O. BOX 13819 MILWAUKEE, WI 53213

www.halleonard.com

P/V/G = Piano/Vocal/Guitar Arrangements

Prices, contents, and availability subject to change without notice.

0415

THE BEST SACRED COLLECTIONS FOR PIANO

The Big Book of Hymns

An invaluable collection of 125 favorite hymns, including: All Hail the Power of Jesus' Name • Battle Hymn of the Republic • Blessed Assurance • For the Beauty of the Earth • Holy, Holy, Holy • It Is Well with My Soul • Just as I Am • A Mighty Fortress Is Our God • The Old Rugged Cross • Onward Christian Soldiers • Rock of Ages • Sweet By and By • What a Friend We Have in Jesus • Wondrous Love • and more.
00310510 P/V/G $17.95

The Best Gospel Songs Ever

80 of the best-loved gospel songs of all time: Amazing Grace • At Calvary • Because He Lives • Behold the Lamb • Daddy Sang Bass • His Eye Is on the Sparrow • His Name Is Wonderful • How Great Thou Art • I Saw the Light • I'll Fly Away • Just a Closer Walk with Thee • Just a Little Talk with Jesus • Mansion over the Hilltop • The Old Rugged Cross • Peace in the Valley • Will the Circle Be Unbroken • Wings of a Dove • more.
00310503 P/V/G $19.99

The Christian Children's Songbook

101 songs from Sunday School, all in appropriate keys for children's voices. Includes: Awesome God • The B-I-B-L-E • Clap Your Hands • Day by Day • He's Got the Whole World in His Hands • Jesus Loves Me • Let There Be Peace on Earth • This Little Light of Mine • more.
00310472 P/V/G $19.95

The Hymn Collection

arranged by Phillip Keveren

17 beloved hymns expertly and beautifully arranged for solo piano by Phillip Keveren. Includes: All Hail the Power of Jesus' Name • I Love to Tell the Story • I Surrender All • I've Got Peace Like a River • Were You There? • and more.
00311071 Piano Solo $11.95

Hymn Duets

arranged by Phillip Keveren

Includes lovely duet arrangements of: All Creatures of Our God and King • I Surrender All • It Is Well with My Soul • O Sacred Head, Now Wounded • Praise to the Lord, The Almighty • Rejoice, The Lord Is King • and more.
00311544 Piano Duet $10.95

P/V/G = Piano/Vocal/Guitar arrangements.
Prices, contents and availability subject to change without notice.

Hymn Medleys

arranged by Phillip Keveren

Great medleys resonate with the human spirit, as do the truths in these moving hymns. Here Phillip Keveren combines 24 timeless favorites into eight lovely medleys for solo piano.
00311349 Piano Solo $10.95

Hymns for Two

arranged by Carol Klose

12 piano duet arrangements of favorite hymns: Amazing Grace • Be Thou My Vision • Crown Him with Many Crowns • Fairest Lord Jesus • Holy, Holy, Holy • I Need Thee Every Hour • O Worship the King • What a Friend We Have in Jesus • and more.
00290544 Piano Duet $10.99

Ragtime Gospel Hymns

arranged by Steven Tedesco

15 traditional gospel hymns, including: At Calvary • Footsteps of Jesus • Just a Closer Walk with Thee • Leaning on the Everlasting Arms • What a Friend We Have in Jesus • When We All Get to Heaven • and more.
00311763 Piano Solo $8.95

Seasonal Sunday Solos for Piano

24 blended selections grouped by occasion. Includes: Breath of Heaven (Mary's Song) • Come, Ye Thankful People, Come • Do You Hear What I Hear • God of Our Fathers • In the Name of the Lord • Mary, Did You Know? • Mighty to Save • Spirit of the Living God • The Wonderful Cross • and more.
00311971 Piano Solo $14.99

Sunday Solos for Piano

30 blended selections, perfect for the church pianist. Songs include: All Hail the Power of Jesus' Name • Be Thou My Vision • Great Is the Lord • Here I Am to Worship • Majesty • Open the Eyes of My Heart • and many more.
00311272 Piano Solo $15.99

More Sunday Solos for Piano

A follow-up to *Sunday Solos for Piano*, this collection features 30 more blended selections perfect for the church pianist. Includes: Agnus Dei • Come, Thou Fount of Every Blessing • The Heart of Worship • How Great Thou Art • Immortal, Invisible • O Worship the King • Shout to the Lord • Thy Word • We Fall Down • and more.
00311864 Piano Solo $14.99

Even More Sunday Solos for Piano

30 blended selections, including: Ancient Words • Brethren, We Have Met to Worship • How Great Is Our God • Lead On, O King Eternal • Offering • Savior, Like a Shepherd Lead Us • We Bow Down • Worthy of Worship • and more.
00312098 Piano Solo $14.99

Solos for Celebrations

These resourceful collections gather and sort songs ideal for various church ceremonies so that musicians can plan services quickly and easily. Includes songs appropriate for baptism and confirmation, church anniversaries and building dedications, commissioning and ordination services, communion, memorial services, and weddings.

Volume 1

24 songs in all, including: Abide with Me • Be Thou My Vision • The Church's One Foundation • Doxology • Here I Am, Lord • How Beautiful • In Christ Alone • Let Us Break Bread Together • O Church Arise • Seekers of Your Heart • To God Be the Glory • Were You There? • What a Friend We Have in Jesus • and more.
00311866 Piano Solo $14.99

Volume 2

Includes: Amazing Grace (My Chains Are Gone) • Blessed Assurance • For All the Saints • Homesick • Household of Faith • I Will Be Here • It Is Well with My Soul • The Lord's Prayer • On Eagle's Wings • Spirit of God, Descend upon My Heart • Stand Up, Stand up for Jesus • We Gather Together • When I Survey the Wondrous Cross • Wondrous Love • and more.
00311867 Piano Solo $14.99

7777 W. BLUEMOUND RD. P.O. BOX 13819 MILWAUKEE, WI 53213
www.halleonard.com

0413